SUPERMAN
SCIENCE

STOPPING RUNAWAY TRAINS

SUPERMAN™ AND THE SCIENCE OF STRENGTH

BY AGNIESZKA BISKUP

SUPERMAN CREATED BY
JERRY SIEGEL
AND JOE SHUSTER
BY SPECIAL ARRANGEMENT
WITH THE JERRY SIEGEL FAMILY

DC COMICS™

T0081116

CAPSTONE PRESS
a capstone imprint

Published by Capstone Press in 2016
A Capstone Imprint
1710 Roe Crest Drive
North Mankato, Minnesota 56003
www.mycapstone.com

STAR36203

Library of Congress Cataloging-in-Publication Data
Names: Biskup, Agnieszka, author.
Title: Stopping runaway trains : Superman and the science of strength / by
   Agnieszka Biskup.
Description: North Mankato, Minnesota : Capstone Press, 2016. | 2016 | Series: DC super
   heroes. Superman science | Audience: Ages 9–12. | Audience: Grade 3 to grade 6. |
   Includes bibliographical references and index.
Identifiers: LCCN 2016002667| ISBN 9781515709145 (library binding) | ISBN 9781515709183
   (paperback) | ISBN 9781515709220 (ebook pdf)
Subjects: LCSH: Muscle strength—Juvenile literature. | Muscles—Juvenile literature. |
   Human physiology—Juvenile literature.
Classification: LCC QP37 .B57 2016 | DDC 612.7/41—dc23
LC record available at http://lccn.loc.gov/2016002667

Summary: Explores the real-world science and engineering related to Superman's
super-strength.

Editorial Credits
Editor: Christopher Harbo
Designer: Bob Lentz
Production Specialist: Tori Abraham
Media Researcher: Eric Gohl

Photo Credits
Dreamstime: Denys Hliuza-Smykovskyi, 18; iStockphoto: oguzaral, 8, pidjoe, 19 (bottom);
Shutterstock: Andrew Bignell, 21 (bottom), BasPhoto, 19 (top), chombosan, 27, chungking,
cover, Designua, 7 (top), 10, digitalbalance, 25 (bottom), dotshock, 12, dwphotos, 13
(bottom), Eduard Kyslynskyy, 22 (bottom), Erik Zandboer, 21 (top), ForeverLee, 9 (bottom),
Henrik Larsson, 25 (top), holbox, 13 (top), James Steidl, 23 (bottom), Joseph Sohm,
20, Luiscar74, 15 (bottom), martan, 9 (top), Nature Art, 23 (top), Nerthuz, 7 (bottom),
Pal2iyawit, 17 (left), Richard Whitcombe, 24, Stefano Cavoretto, 14, stihii, 11 (top),
Vereshchagin Dmitry, 28, Ververidis Vasilis, 17 (right), vitstudio, 11 (bottom), Volodymyr
Burdiak, 22 (top), Yeko Photo Studio, 15 (top), Zzvet, 29

Printed in the United States of America in North Mankato, Minnesota.
009667F16

TABLE OF CONTENTS

T |||∙⊆Ω

STRONGER THAN STEEL

Superman's strength is legendary. He can bend thick steel beams with his bare hands. He can lift subway cars, airplanes, and oil tankers. He can even crush diamonds in his fist. But if you think amazing feats of strength are limited to the Man of Steel, think again. Strength is at work just about everywhere you look.

Take your own body for example. Every single move you make—from picking up a pencil to carrying a backpack—depends on your muscles. You have hundreds of muscles in your body and they allow you to move in thousands of different ways. Some people train their muscles to be stronger or faster. Others teach them to do delicate things such as perform surgery or play the violin.

But the science of strength is about more than just muscles. From powerful animals to strength-boosting technology, our world is loaded with examples of incredible strength. Get ready to explore how strength plays a part in just about everything we do.

FACT:

The very first comic book featuring Superman showcased his incredible strength. The cover of the 1938 *Action Comics* #1 showed him lifting a car above his head.

HUMAN STRENGTH

Superman gets his strength by absorbing the energy from Earth's yellow Sun. But his muscles still work much like the ones in our bodies.

WHAT'S A MUSCLE?

Muscles are the parts of your body that create movement. They either move things inside your body, such as blood and food, or move the body itself. In fact, your body has more than 600 muscles. They make up roughly 30 to 50 percent of your weight.

The three main types of muscles are smooth, cardiac, and skeletal. Smooth muscles are also called **involuntary** muscles. Why? Because they often move without you telling them to. Smooth muscles move food through your intestines, push air through your lungs, and even help your eyes focus.

Cardiac muscle is very specialized. It's only found in your heart. The heart is a muscle that pumps blood throughout your body. Just like some smooth muscles, it works all by itself with no help from you.

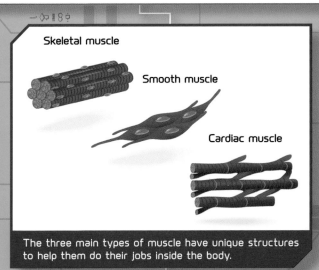

Skeletal muscle

Smooth muscle

Cardiac muscle

The three main types of muscle have unique structures to help them do their jobs inside the body.

The muscles you probably think about most are skeletal muscles. These can move, push, pull, and lift. Skeletal muscles are **voluntary**, which means they move the way you tell them to. They help you walk, run, throw a ball, and turn the pages of this book.

FACT:

Eye muscles are the busiest in the body. They may move more than 100,000 times a day.

involuntary—done without a person's control

voluntary—done on purpose and not by accident

THE MUSCULOSKELETAL SYSTEM

Skeletal muscles work with your bones to make up your musculoskeletal system. To provide power and strength, skeletal muscles must be connected to something solid to move your body. That something solid is bone. Imagine a runner pushing off a starting block to begin a race. Just like runners, muscles need a solid object on which to push or pull.

Most muscles are connected to bones by stiff, stringlike fibers called tendons. Some tendons are very long, allowing a muscle to move a bone that's far away. For instance, long tendons connected to muscles attached to your elbow help your fingers move. Other tendons are tiny, such as the ones in your ears and eyes.

MUSCLE

TENDONS

Tendons connect muscles to bones.

FACT:

The biggest muscle in your body is the one you sit on. The gluteus maximus is just a fancy scientific name for your butt muscle.

Muscles cover your body in layers—and most bones have more than one muscle attached to them. The reason is simple. A single muscle can usually only work in one direction. You need multiple muscles to move in different directions.

Layers of muscles cover the body from head to toe.

MUSCLE SHAPES

Skeletal muscles come in many shapes and sizes to allow them to do different things. The muscles around your mouth are circular to allow it to open and close, whistle, or kiss. The deltoids in your shoulders are triangular. They need to be thicker where they attach to your shoulder blades. They are thinner where they attach to your arm.

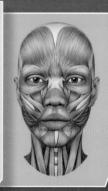

HOW MUSCLES WORK

When Superman keeps a skyscraper from toppling over, it's easy to be awed by his strength. But just like us, he has muscles under his skin. And whether muscles are superpowered or just human-powered, the science behind how they work is pretty remarkable.

Skeletal muscles are made up of fibers that line up next to each other in bundles. These muscle fibers contract and stretch, allowing your body to move. Contraction makes a muscle shorter. When a muscle gets shorter, it pulls on the bone attached to it.

Skeletal muscle

Consider the biceps on top of your upper arm, for example. This muscle attaches to the bones around your elbow and your shoulder blade. When you lift a glass of water, your biceps contracts to pull your arm up. To put the glass down, you use the triceps located under your upper arm. This muscle contracts to lower your arm—and the glass—back to the table.

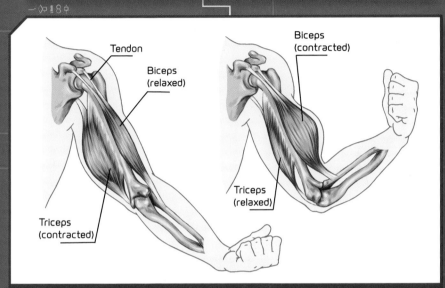

Tendon

Biceps (relaxed)

Biceps (contracted)

Triceps (relaxed)

Triceps (contracted)

The triceps and biceps work as a team to move your arm up and down.

BRAIN SIGNALS

How do your arm muscles know you want to lift an object? Your brain sends signals through nerves in the muscle fibers. The nerves tell the muscles to contract by sending electrical impulses. That's why an electrical shock makes your muscles twitch without you telling them to.

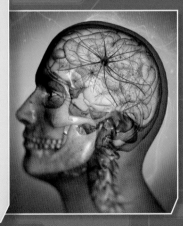

nerve—a thin fiber that carries messages between the brain and other parts of the body

ENHANCING STRENGTH

Superman doesn't need to go to the gym to get huge muscles and incredible strength. Our yellow Sun's energy gives him the power boost he needs. For the rest of us, enhancing our strength takes exercise.

STRENGTH TRAINING

Regular exercise is great for your muscles, but it may not make you look like a super hero. For that, you need strength training. This type of exercise uses **resistance** to make muscles work harder.

To feel how resistance makes your muscles work harder, try this simple test. Curl your arm while holding a small dumbbell. Can you feel your biceps working harder than normal? Now repeat the curling motion 10 more times. Is your arm getting tired? That means you're pushing your muscles to work harder. The more times you repeat an exercise, the harder your muscles must work. The harder they work, the stronger they become.

Dumbell curls strengthen the biceps.

Strength training can be done with your own body weight, resistance bands, free weights, and weight machines. Body weight strength training uses your own body's weight to create resistance. Common body weight exercises include push-ups, pull-ups, sit-ups, and leg squats. Resistance bands are long, lightweight bands that create resistance when you stretch them. Free weights include barbells and dumbbells. Weight machines have built-in weights or resistance bands to exercise specific muscles in the body.

Push-ups use the body's own weight to strengthen muscles in the arms.

MYOSTATIN AND MUSCLES

Almost every animal on Earth produces myostatin. This protein limits the size muscles can grow. But some animals, including mice and cattle, are born with a myostatin disorder. Their levels of myostatin are so low that they grow massive muscles without any strength training at all.

resistance—a force that opposes or slows the motion of an object

protein—a chemical made by animal and plant cells to carry out various functions

BODYBUILDING

Regular strength training is a good start to building a super hero body. But to really get the job done, weight training is the key. It's the type of strength training bodybuilders use to try to look as muscular as Superman.

Bodybuilders don't just build strength, they train specific muscles to maximize their size and shape. To do this, bodybuilders steadily increase the weight they lift as they train. These increases are necessary because muscles get used to exercise. If a bodybuilder always lifted the same weight, his or her muscles wouldn't get any bigger. But increasing the weight they lift actually causes tiny tears in their muscles. As their bodies repair these tears, bodybuilders' muscles bulk up.

Bodybuilders use weight training to sculpt their muscles.

FACT:

Actor and former California governor Arnold Schwarzenegger started out as a bodybuilder. He won titles at five Mr. Universe and seven Mr. Olympia bodybuilding competitions.

Bodybuilders use weight machines to help train specific muscle groups.

ANABOLIC STEROIDS

Our bodies make a hormone called testosterone that helps build muscle. Anabolic steroids are man-made versions of testosterone. Doctors sometimes prescribe these steroids to help people regain body mass after an illness. But some athletes, bodybuilders, and others take them illegally to increase muscle mass and strength. Anabolic steroid abuse can have extremely dangerous side effects, including liver and heart problems.

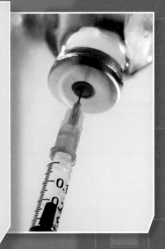

hormone—a chemical made by a gland in the body that affects growth and development

mass—the amount of material in an object

FEATS OF STRENGTH

People have been fascinated by feats of strength for thousands of years. Long before Superman, Greek and Roman myths featured the tales of Hercules, the world's most famous strongman. It's no wonder, then, that modern feats of strength continue to capture our imaginations today.

WEIGHTLIFTERS

Some of today's most impressive feats of strength happen in the Olympic Games. Nowhere is this more true than in the sport of weightlifting, where men and women compete by hefting incredible weights above their heads.

Olympic weightlifters compete using two types of lifts: the clean-and-jerk and the snatch. The clean-and-jerk is made up of two movements. During the "clean," lifters move the barbell from the floor to their collarbones. During the "jerk," the lifters raise the barbell above their heads, with straight arms and legs. For the snatch, the goal is to lift a barbell from the ground and overhead in one continuous motion.

clean-and-jerk

snatch

WEIGHTLIFTING RECORD-HOLDERS

Hossein Rezazadeh from Iran holds the current men's Olympic record for both the snatch and the clean-and-jerk. He lifted 467 pounds (212 kg) using the snatch. He hoisted 580 pounds (263 kg) using the clean-and-jerk. For women, Tatiana Kashirina of Russia holds the current Olympic record for the snatch at 333 pounds (151 kg). Lulu Zhou of China holds the clean-and-jerk record at 412 pounds (187 kg).

myth—a story told by people in ancient times

THE WORLD'S STRONGEST MAN

Olympic weightlifting isn't the only competition that pushes the limits of the human body. The World's Strongest Man competition tests competitors' strength with a variety of unusual events. Among them are the Farmer's Walk and the Atlas Stones.

In the Farmer's Walk, competitors carry two 353-pound (160-kg) weights. The goal is to move them a set distance within a certain amount of time. Competitors can set down and pick up the weights as many times as they like. But the one who completes the walk with the fastest time wins the event.

A strongman competitor prepares to lift two barbells in a Farmer's Walk event.

FACT:

In Greek mythology, Atlas is a Titan who holds up the sky. During his adventures, Hercules once held up the sky in Atlas' place.

Atlas

The Atlas Stones event features five round stones. The lightest weighs 220 pounds (100 kg). The heaviest weighs 353 pounds (160 kg). Competitors need to pick up and place these massive stones on five high platforms on a 16- to 33-foot (5- to 10-meter) course. The person who completes the course the fastest wins.

ARM WRESTLING

In arm wrestling, winners and losers are decided by whose muscle fibers can fire simultaneously the fastest. The *Guinness Book of World Records* lists John Brzenk as the Greatest Arm Wrestler of All Time. He is known for easily pinning opponents twice his size. The heaviest opponent he defeated weighed 660 pounds (299 kg). That was more than twice Brzenk's weight.

ANIMAL STRENGTH

When super-villains wreak havoc on the world, Superman's incredible strength is often the difference between life and death. In the animal world, strength plays an important role in how animals survive in their environments too. Large and small, animals flex their muscles in remarkable ways.

BIG AND STRONG

In the animal world, brute strength is all about size. You've probably heard the saying "strong as an ox." The phrase exists for a reason. Oxen are huge, making them the go-to work animal for thousands of years. An ox is so strong it can pull about one and a half times its body weight. A team of oxen working together can pull thousands of pounds. No wonder they were historically used to plow fields, haul wagons, and power machines to grind grain.

oxen

Gorillas, the world's largest **primates**, are no slouches in terms of brute strength either. Males can be 5 feet 9 inches (1.75 m) tall and weigh 440 pounds (200 kg). They are believed to have about six times more upper body strength than an average man. A gorilla can lift objects that weigh 4,400 pounds (2,000 kg). That's 10 times its body weight!

gorilla

Not to be outdone, Bengal tigers—the biggest members of the cat family—are known for impressive strength too. After a kill, they often drag their meal to a hiding place. One Bengal tiger was seen dragging an adult gaur 40 feet (12.2 m). An average adult gaur weighs 2,000 pounds (907 kg)!

Bengal tiger

primate—any member of the group of intelligent animals that includes humans, apes, and monkeys

BIGGER AND EVEN STRONGER

Superman is famous for stopping runaway trains. But did you know some animals on Earth might have enough strength to do the same? In fact, in the 1890s an elephant reportedly charged and derailed a train to protect its herd.

An elephant derailing a train is easy to imagine when you stop to consider its size. African elephants are the largest land animals on the planet. They can grow about 13 feet (4 m) tall at the shoulder and weigh up to 14,000 pounds (6,350 kg). An elephant that size can carry almost 20,000 pounds (9,070 kg). Even more impressive, an African elephant's flexible trunk has tens of thousands of muscles. It can lift 770 pounds (349 kg)—or the weight of three large men together—with its trunk alone!

African elephant

Blue whales can grow longer than two double-decker buses parked end-to-end.

Elephants may be the largest land animals, but blue whales are the largest animals to ever live on Earth. They measure up to 100 feet (30 m) long and weigh up to 200 tons (181 metric tons). That's longer than two double-decker buses end-to-end, and as heavy as about 28 elephants! As the largest animals alive, their muscles can generate a huge amount of force. In 2014 a blue whale tipped over a 21-foot- (6.4-m-) long boat off the coast of California.

STRONG AND TINY

Amazing strength isn't limited to big animals. One of the strongest animals in the world for its size is the mantis shrimp. This 4-inch- (10-cm-) long sea creature packs a punch with the speed of a .22 caliber bullet. It uses its club-like body parts to break the shells of the crabs and snails it eats. When the shrimp releases its clubs, they **accelerate** to 50 miles (80 km) per hour. Where does all this power come from? The clubs are spring loaded, like a crossbow. Aquarium tanks have to be made of especially strong plastic because these tiny shrimp can actually shatter glass!

mantis shrimp

horned dung beetle

Mantis shrimp aren't the only mighty mini-creatures in the world. The strongest insect on the planet is the horned dung beetle. Yes, it feeds on dung—but what it can pull is even more amazing than what it eats for lunch. The horned dung beetle can pull 1,141 times its own body weight. That would be like a person pulling 180,000 pounds (81,640 kg), or six double-decker buses. Now that's one strong bug!

STRONGEST JUMPER

The tiny copepod is the world's strongest jumper. This crustacean is barely 0.04 inch (1 mm) long. But its jumping muscles are 10 times more forceful than any other animal's on Earth. A 5-foot 8-inch (173-cm) tall person leaping with the same power would top out at 3,800 miles (6,115 km) per hour!

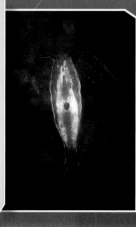

accelerate—to increase the speed of a moving object

FUTURE STRENGTH

People can only dream about having Superman's strength. But if scientists and engineers get their way, those dreams may one day become a reality. Check out the exciting ways science and technology might enhance strength in our world.

EXOSKELETONS

If you had Superman's X-ray vision, you'd see the skeletons inside people's bodies. But did you know some animals, such as insects and crustaceans, have skeletons on the outside of their bodies? These exoskeletons have inspired scientists and engineers with ways to boost human strength.

Human exoskeletons have already been developed for the military. Lockheed Martin's Human Universal Load Carrier (HULC) is designed to help soldiers carry heavy loads in combat. The HULC exoskeleton straps onto a soldier's thighs, waist, and shoulders. Once on, the weight of a soldier's gear is transferred to the device's **titanium** legs. The HULC allows users to carry up to 200-pound (91-kg) loads with very little stress on the body.

Robotic exoskeletons allow people to lift heavy loads with very little effort and a low risk of injury.

The HULC isn't the only exoskeleton being developed for the military. Raytheon Sarcos' XOS 2 is a full-body robotics suit for soldiers. It allows users to repeatedly lift 200 pounds (91 kg) of weight without getting tired. It's also strong enough to easily punch through 3 inches (76 mm) of wood. Engineers believe that one soldier wearing the XOS 2 can do the work of up to three regular soldiers.

titanium—a very strong and light metal

The military isn't the only place where strength enhancement is the wave of the future. The medical field is also looking for ways to increase strength—both outside and inside the body.

While exoskeletons can help soldiers carry heavy loads, they can also help people who are **paralyzed** from the waist down. Ekso Bionics and ReWalk Robotics have already developed battery-powered exoskeletons for people with spinal cord injuries. These devices provide hip and knee motion to help people stand and walk. In 2012, a ReWalk helped Claire Lomas, who is paralyzed from the chest down, complete the London Marathon.

A battery-powered exoskeleton helps a woman walk.

paralyzed—unable to move or feel a part of the body

gene—a part of every cell that carries physical and behavioral information passed from parents to their children

Strength enhancement is also being studied on the microscopic level. Scientists hope to treat muscle diseases by changing the **genes** that cause them. In fact, genetic engineering may change us more than any other technology in the future. For instance, scientists at Ohio State University and Nationwide Children's Hospital have changed a gene in macaque monkeys. It lets their muscles grow about 25 percent larger and stronger than normal.

macaque

CONCLUSION

When it comes to strength, everyone looks up to Superman. The Man of Steel can lift, carry, push, and pull more than any mortal man or woman. And even though we may never reach his level of greatness, he inspires us to test our limits and explore our potential. With the science of strength, we may one day have the might to move mountains too.

GLOSSARY

accelerate (ak-SEL-uh-rayt)—to increase the speed of a moving object

gene (JEEN)—a part of every cell that carries physical and behavioral information passed from parents to their children

hormone (HOR-mohn)—a chemical made by a gland in the body that affects growth and development

involuntary (in-VOL-uhn-tehr-ee)—done without a person's control

mass (MASS)—the amount of material in an object

myth (MITH)—a story told by people in ancient times

nerve (NURV)—a thin fiber that carries messages between the brain and other parts of the body

paralyzed (PA-ruh-lized)—unable to move or feel a part of the body

primate (PRYE-mate)—any member of the group of intelligent animals that includes humans, apes, and monkeys

protein (PROH-teen)—a chemical made by animal and plant cells to carry out various functions

resistance (ri-ZISS-tuhnss)—a force that opposes or slows the motion of an object

titanium (tahy-TEY-nee-uhm)—a very strong and light metal

voluntary (VOL-uhn-ter-ee)—done on purpose and not by accident

READ MORE

Fittleworth, George. *Your Muscles*. Know Your Body. New York: Gareth Stevens Publishing, 2017.

Halvorson, Karin. *Inside the Muscles*. Super Simple Body. Minneapolis: ABDO Publishing, 2016.

Mooney, Carla. *Wearable Robots*. Tech Bytes. Chicago: Norwood Press, 2016.

Scott, Celicia. *Weight Lifting & Strength Building*. An Integrated Life of Fitness. Broomall, Penn.: Mason Crest, 2015.

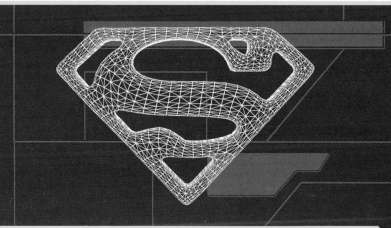

INTERNET SITES

FactHound offers a safe, fun way to find Internet sites related to this book. All of the sites on FactHound have been researched by our staff.

Here's all you do:

Visit *www.facthound.com*

Type in this code: 9781515709145

INDEX